PIVOT WITH PURPOSE

THRIVING THROUGH LIFE'S TRANSITIONS

ADIA THOMPSON WHITE

Copyright

DEDICATION

This book is dedicated to the woman who finds
herself standing at a crossroads, unsure of what's
next. My prayer is that you find peace in the
process, perspective in the pause, and purpose in
your pivot.

CONTENTS

Introduction: The Art of the Pivot   **7**

NAVIGATING LIFE'S TRANSITIONS

Chapter 1.
The College-to-Career Pivot   13

Chapter 2.
The New Motherhood Pivot   17

Chapter 3.
The Career Change Pivot   21

Chapter 4.
The Empty Nest Pivot   25

Chapter 5.
The Retirement Pivot   29

FOUNDATIONS FOR THRIVING

Chapter 6.
Thoughts: Reframing the Story You Tell Yourself   35

Chapter 7.
Health & Wellness: Leading with Energy, Not Exhaustion   41

Chapter 8.
Resilience: Bouncing Back and Rising Higher   47

Chapter 9.
Identity: Rediscovering Who You Are Beyond the Roles   53

Chapter 10.
Vision: Designing the Next Chapter with Intention   57

Chapter 11.
Execution: Turning Vision into Courageous Action   61

THRIVING IN COMMUNITY & LEADERSHIP

Chapter 12.
Faith, Purpose, and Calling: Anchoring in Something Bigger   67

Chapter 13.
The Power of Community and Sisterhood   71

MASTERING THE PIVOT WITH THRIVE

Chapter 14.
The Pivot Playbook: Applying THRIVE to Any Transition   77

Chapter 15.
Common Detours and How to Get Back on Track   83

Chapter 16.
Thriving Beyond the Pivot: Creating a Life You Love   87

Acknowledgements   91

INTRODUCTION:
THE ART OF THE PIVOT

I know what it feels like to stand at a crossroads. To feel the ground shift beneath your feet and wonder, *what now?*

A major pivot in my career occurred after I had spent years working in nonprofit and corporate spaces, climbing the ladder, earning promotions, and checking the boxes of what "success" was supposed to look like. At one point, I was being groomed as my manager's replacement. The next step was practically guaranteed. Except for one thing: the person I would be reporting to was toxic. She belittled staff in meetings, reneged on commitments, and created an atmosphere of fear.

When an opportunity came my way, I had a choice: take the safe promotion or choose myself. I walked away.

That wasn't the only pivot. Like millions of women, I was laid off at the beginning of the COVID pandemic. At first, I felt the sting of loss. But in that season, I also discovered resilience in ways I hadn't expected. I leaned on my village. I created a community. I found beauty in nature, walking outside daily. I rediscovered my love for planning. And I began helping other women who, like me, were searching for the courage to reimagine their next chapter.

These pivots taught me something I now teach every client, audience, and leader I work with: **a pivot is not just a detour, it's an invitation.**

Insight

Transitions are universal. For women, they take many forms:

- College to career
- Becoming a mother
- Changing careers mid-life
- Children leaving the nest
- Retirement and legacy-building

At each pivot, women are faced with unique pressures: self-doubt, caregiving expectations, bias in the workplace, burnout, financial insecurity, or loss of identity. Studies show:

- **75% of women** experience imposter syndrome in their careers (KPMG).
- **43% of highly qualified women** leave or scale back work after childbirth (Harvard Business Review).
- **Women have about 30% less saved for retirement** than men and face a 32% lower median income after age 65, leaving them more vulnerable in later life. (Morgan Stanley)

But pivots are also opportunities. They are moments to shed old expectations and step into a life built on clarity, purpose, and thriving.

This is where my THRIVE Framework comes in. THRIVE is not just a catchy acronym. It's the structure I've lived, tested, and taught:

T Thoughts: Reframing your mindset to overcome doubt and embrace possibility.

Your thoughts shape your reality. By shifting limiting beliefs into empowering truths, you create space for growth and courage in every transition.

H Health & Wellness: Protecting your energy, strengthening your body, and renewing your mind.

Thriving isn't possible without wellbeing. Prioritizing rhythms of rest, movement, and nourishment ensures you can sustain purpose and joy.

R Resilience: Rising stronger after setbacks and learning to adapt with grace.

Life will bring challenges, but resilience helps you bounce back wiser, grounded, and ready to keep moving forward.

I Identity: Embracing who you truly are, beyond roles and expectations.

Thriving means showing up authentically. When you lead from your true identity, you inspire connection, confidence, and clarity.

V Vision: Designing your future with clarity and intention.

Every pivot is an invitation to dream again. Vision provides direction, helping you align today's choices with tomorrow's purpose.

E Execution: Turning clarity into consistent, courageous action.

Dreams without action remain ideas. Execution is where vision meets discipline and where you commit to the steps that make thriving a reality.

Reflection Prompts

1. Think back to the last major transition in your life. Did it feel like a loss, an opportunity, or both?
2. What story did you tell yourself in that moment?
3. What part of you grew stronger because of it?

Tool: Your Pivot Audit

Take 10 minutes to answer these questions in your journal:

1. What transition am I currently navigating (or anticipating)?
2. What emotions come up when I think about it?
3. What do I believe this transition is teaching me?
4. What kind of support or framework would help me thrive through it?

Keep this pivot audit handy. As you move through this book, you'll revisit it after each chapter, adding new insights and strategies to carry you forward.

PART I

NAVIGATING LIFE'S TRANSITIONS

CHAPTER 1

The College-to-Career Pivot

I'll never forget the season after graduation, the excitement of finishing my degree, mixed with the fear of not knowing exactly where I was headed next.

In college, there's a sense of identity and structure. You know the rhythm: classes, exams, friends, activities. But stepping into your first job (or searching for one) can feel like standing on shaky ground. Suddenly, you're in boardrooms instead of classrooms. You're expected to know how to navigate office politics, manage your finances, and make adult decisions.

For many young women, this is where imposter syndrome first rears its ugly head. You wonder if you really belong in that role, if your voice matters, if you're enough compared to the seasoned professionals around you.

This chapter is for every woman stepping into her first career, figuring out who she is outside of a campus, and learning how to thrive in this new season.

Insight

The transition from college to career is one of the most critical pivots in a woman's life. It sets the tone for confidence, earning potential, and future opportunities.

Research highlights both the challenges and opportunities:

- 75% of women experience imposter syndrome in their careers. (KPMG, *Mind the Gap*)
- More than half of college graduates are underemployed in their first job. (Inside Higher Ed)
- Women typically earn 82 cents for every dollar men earn. (Pew Research Center)

These realities show why the college-to-career transition is not just about landing a job; it's about building the confidence, resilience, and clarity to navigate systemic challenges while shaping a career that aligns with your values.

 Pivot Story Spotlight

Taylor graduated with honors in communications but couldn't find a job in her field right away. So, she took an administrative assistant role just to pay the bills. At first, she felt like she had failed. But instead of giving up, she leaned on mentors, joined a young professionals' network, and kept building her skills.

Within three years, Taylor leveraged that early job into a marketing manager role at a national nonprofit.

"It wasn't where I thought I'd start," she said, "but the experience I gained taught me persistence, humility, and how to advocate for myself."

Taylor's story reminds us that your first job doesn't define your whole career. Every step can be a stepping stone toward something greater.

Reflection Prompts

1. What fears do I have about starting my career?
2. What skills or strengths do I bring into the workplace that give me confidence?
3. Who can I reach out to for mentorship or guidance in this season?
4. If I could design my ideal career, what would it look like in 5 years?

The First 90 Days Plan

Here's a framework to help you thrive in your first job or new role:

1. **Learn the Landscape**
   - Spend your first weeks observing. Who holds influence? How does communication flow? What unspoken rules shape the culture?

2. **Build Relationships**
   - Schedule coffee chats with colleagues or mentors. Ask questions, listen well, and begin building your professional network.

3. **Demonstrate Value**
   - Look for quick wins, small projects you can complete well to establish credibility early.

4. **Ask for Feedback**
   - Don't wait for annual reviews. Ask your manager and peers how you're doing and how you can improve during regular check-ins.

5. **Invest in Yourself**
   - Continue learning through workshops, courses, or certifications. Your growth shouldn't stop at graduation.

Closing Encouragement

The college-to-career pivot is both thrilling and terrifying. But **you don't have to have it all figured out on day one.**

Your first job doesn't define your entire career. It's a launchpad. It's a place to learn, grow, and build the confidence that will carry you into future opportunities.

Show up. Speak up. Be willing to learn. And remember that you belong in the room and are prepared to grow.

CHAPTER 2

The New Motherhood Pivot

When I became a mother, my world shifted overnight.

I still remember the day we brought Jalyn home from the hospital. I was in pain (still recovering from a c-section), terrified, and filled with love all at the same time. In those first weeks, my days blurred into a cycle of feeding, changing, soothing, and praying that she would sleep just a little longer.

When Kendall came along nearly five years later, the juggling act multiplied. Now it wasn't just work and home, I had two little ones depending on me, a career that demanded my best, and the constant feeling that no matter what I did, something (or someone) was being neglected.

Motherhood is beautiful. But it can also be overwhelming.

I felt pressure to perform everywhere. At home, I wanted to be the perfect mom. At work, I felt like I had to prove I was still committed and capable. Inside, I wondered: *Am I enough? Can I do this without losing myself?*

I wasn't alone. Many women feel this tension, the joy of motherhood coupled with the fear of losing their identity or career in the process. This chapter is about learning how to pivot into motherhood with grace, support, and the reminder that you don't have to do it all alone.

Insight

Motherhood is one of the most profound transitions women experience. It's both an identity shift and a lifestyle shift.

Research shows the challenges clearly:

- 43% of highly qualified women leave or scale back their careers after having children. (The Atlantic)
- 1 in 3 mothers considered leaving or downshifting their careers during the pandemic due to burnout and lack of support. (Lean In)
- Motherhood triggers identity shifts as women renegotiate professional, personal, and domestic roles. (Journal of Reproductive and Infant Psychology)

These statistics reveal what so many mothers feel: becoming a parent often comes with pressure to step back, fit into new expectations, or reorient your entire life around your children.

But **motherhood doesn't erase who you are; it expands it.**

When women are supported through this transition (at home, in the workplace, and in the community), they not only raise thriving families but they also thrive themselves.

 *Pivot Story Spotlight*

Lisa was a new mom working in a demanding law firm. She loved her baby, but she also loved her career. Within months, she found herself drowning in guilt. When she stayed late at work, she felt she was failing at home. When she left early, she worried that her colleagues would see her as less committed.

Through coaching, Lisa realized she didn't have to choose between motherhood and professional fulfillment. She just had to redefine success for this season. She set boundaries around her work hours, renegotiated some responsibilities with her spouse, and gave herself permission to be a good enough mom instead of a perfect one.

Her shift in perspective gave her space to breathe and reminded her that thriving in motherhood is about balance, not perfection.

Reflection Prompts

1. What expectations am I carrying about motherhood, my own or others?
2. Where am I feeling the most pressure to "do it all"?
3. What rhythms or supports could help me feel more balanced?
4. How has motherhood changed my sense of identity, for better or for worse?

Tool: The Balance Audit

Here's a simple way to identify where you need more support and where you can reclaim energy.

Step 1: List Your Buckets
Write down your main roles right now (e.g., mother, professional, partner, friend, daughter).

Step 2: Score Your Energy
Next to each role, score from 1–10: How energized vs. drained do I feel in this role?

Step 3: Identify What's Missing
For roles that feel draining, ask: What would make this feel lighter? (e.g., childcare help, flexible work, sharing house responsibilities).

Step 4: Take One Action
Pick ONE small change to make this week.

- Example: Ask your partner to take over bedtime 2 nights a week.

- Example: Block one afternoon for uninterrupted work.

Step 5: Revisit and Adjust
Do a Balance Audit every month. Notice how your energy shifts and adjust as needed.

Closing Encouragement

Motherhood is one of the greatest pivots you'll ever make. It will stretch you, change you, and sometimes exhaust you. But it will also expand your heart and your vision of what's possible.

You don't have to do this alone. Lean on your support system. Redefine success for your season. Give yourself permission to be both a devoted mother and a thriving woman.

Motherhood isn't about losing yourself. It's about becoming even more of who you were meant to be.

CHAPTER 3

The Career Change Pivot

Midway through my career, I was being groomed to step into a senior leadership role. On paper, it looked like the perfect next step: more influence, more responsibility, and the kind of promotion that others worked years to achieve.

But there was a problem: the CEO was toxic.

I watched as he publicly berated staff, broke commitments, and created a culture of fear. I knew that if I stepped into the role, I'd inherit not just a title but also an environment that would slowly erode my health, my joy, and my sense of purpose.

So, I did something people thought was unthinkable: When another opportunity arose, I walked away.

Leaving that job wasn't easy. I had doubts. Would another opportunity come? Would people think I couldn't handle leadership? Was I risking too much? But deep down, I knew that staying would cost me more.

That pivot became one of the most defining moves of my career. It reminded me that success isn't just about climbing higher, it's about climbing in the right direction.

Insight

Career change is one of the most common pivots women make. Some choose it. Others have it forced upon them. Either way, it can feel overwhelming.

Here's what the research shows:

- Nearly half of all Americans are considering a career change (Forbes)
- Women are more likely to leave jobs for culture, lack of flexibility, or misalignment with values, not just salary. (McKinsey, *Women in the Workplace 2022*)
- Burnout is one of the top drivers of career change, with women more likely than men to report it. (Lean In, *Women in the Workplace 2021*)

Together, these findings paint a clear picture that women pivot for better lives.

A career change is rarely just about leaving a job. It's about reclaiming alignment, health, and purpose.

————————  *Pivot Story Spotlight* ————————

Jasmine had built a successful career in finance but every morning she dreaded going to work. She was good at what she did, however, the long hours and cutthroat culture left her drained.

"I felt like I was living someone else's dream," she confessed.

Through coaching, Jasmine realized her true passion was in education. It wasn't an overnight switch. She took classes, volunteered, and built a network in the nonprofit sector. Within two years, she transitioned into a leadership role at an educational foundation.

"I make less money now," Jasmine said, "but I feel richer than I ever have."

Her story reminds us that career pivots aren't always easy, but when you align your work with your values, you gain a different kind of wealth.

Reflection Prompts

1. What aspects of my current career feel aligned with my values? Which feels misaligned?
2. What fears come up when I think about making a career change?
3. How would my life look different if my work energized me instead of drained me?
4. Who can I talk to (mentors, peers, coaches) to help me explore new possibilities?

Tool: The Career Pivot Compass

This tool helps you evaluate if a career pivot is right for you and how to move forward with clarity.

Step 1: Assess Alignment
Draw a circle divided into four sections: *Values, Strengths, Interests, and Lifestyle.* Score your current role in each area (1–10).

Step 2: Identify the Gaps
Which areas score lowest? Where is the misalignment?

Step 3: Explore Possibilities
Brainstorm roles or industries where your values, strengths, and interests might overlap more fully.

Step 4: Take Small Tests
Before leaping, test. Take a class, shadow someone, volunteer, or freelance in the new field.

Step 5: Create a Transition Plan
Decide: What do I need (financial, skills, network) to make the change? Set a 6–12 month timeline.

Step 6: Revisit Regularly
Check in monthly. Is your current role becoming less tolerable? Is your future role becoming clearer? Adjust accordingly.

Closing Encouragement

It takes strength to walk away from a career that no longer serves you and step toward something uncertain but aligned.

If you're standing at the edge of a career shift, remember that you don't need to have the entire path mapped out. You just need the courage to take the next step.

Thriving in your career isn't about chasing titles but about pursuing alignment. And when your work reflects your values, your whole life flourishes.

CHAPTER 4

The Empty Nest Pivot

As a young mother, I couldn't imagine being an empty nester, no longer hearing the constant rhythm of the girls' comings and goings.

For years, my identity has been intertwined with being Mom. Letting go is bittersweet. Of course, they'll always need me but in a different way. And I'm rediscovering who I am in this new season, beyond being the daily parenting.

The empty nest isn't just about children leaving home. It's about parents, especially mothers, navigating a profound shift in identity, purpose, and rhythm. It's a pivot that can feel like a loss but also an opportunity for renewal.

Insight

The "empty nest" transition is often romanticized as a time of freedom. However, research shows it can be deeply challenging, especially for women whose identity has been strongly tied to caregiving.

- Empty nest syndrome is associated with sadness, loss of purpose, and identity stress for many women as children leave home. (**Journal of Education and Health Promotion**)

- Female empty nesters often report poorer physical and mental health compared to men, especially when social participation is low. (**Frontiers in Public Health**)

The empty nest is not a pivot point in health, identity, and purpose. It can also be an invitation to rediscover passions long set aside, invest in relationships with a partner or friends, and design a vision for what comes next.

 *Pivot Story Spotlight*

Linda had poured her life into raising three children. When her youngest left for college, she felt lost.

"I woke up and didn't know what to do with myself," she admitted. "For so long, my schedule was their schedule."

Instead of staying in that place of loss, Linda decided to reclaim parts of herself she had set aside. She enrolled in a painting class, started volunteering at a local nonprofit, and even planned a trip with her husband that they had been putting off for years.

"Now," she said with a smile, "I'm not just filling time. I'm building a new season that feels like mine."

Reflection Prompts

1. How do I feel when I picture life after my children leave home?

2. What roles or activities have I put aside that I'd love to revisit?

3. How can I nurture my marriage, friendships, or community in this season?

4. What vision do I want to create for this next chapter of life?

Tool: The Rediscovery Plan

This exercise will help you embrace the empty nest as an opportunity for growth.

Step 1: Name the Loss
Acknowledge what feels hard (such as loneliness, loss of routine, and identity shifts). Write it down.

Step 2: Identify Dormant Dreams
List passions, hobbies, or goals you've put aside during active parenting.

Step 3: Explore New Possibilities
What new opportunities does this season make possible? Travel, education, leadership, community involvement?

Step 4: Create a Connection Map
Who do you want to deepen relationships with in this season (partner, siblings, friends, colleagues)?

Step 5: Design a Weekly Rhythm
Block time for rediscovery, whether that's joining a club, taking classes, or dedicating evenings to a creative pursuit.

Closing Encouragement

The empty nest is the beginning of a new chapter. Yes, it comes with grief. But it also comes with freedom, space, and the opportunity to rediscover who you are beyond motherhood.

So, if you're approaching this pivot, give yourself permission to feel the loss and then embrace the invitation.

The empty nest doesn't mean life is smaller. It means life is ready to expand in new ways.

CHAPTER 5

The Retirement Pivot

When I imagine retirement, I don't picture a gold watch, a farewell cake, or walking out of an office for the last time. I picture a blank canvas.

For decades, work has given us structure. The alarm clocks. The commutes. The meetings. The projects. Then suddenly, the calendar is empty. The structure is gone. And for many women, that shift feels less like freedom and more like free fall.

I remember talking with a colleague years ago who had just retired. She had been a powerhouse at her organization, respected, accomplished, the kind of woman who made things happen. But when I asked her how she was adjusting, she sighed.

"Everyone congratulated me, but nobody told me how lonely it would feel," she said. "I went from being needed every day to wondering if anyone even noticed I wasn't there."

Her words stuck with me. Retirement is about stepping away from an identity you've carried for decades and figuring out who you are without it.

That blank canvas can become whatever you design. A season of rest. A season of rediscovery. A season of giving back. Retirement is not an ending, it's a pivot into a new kind of purpose.

Insight

Retirement is one of the biggest pivots women face. And for many, it's layered with both financial and emotional complexity.

Research shows:

- Women retire with about 30% less savings and 32% lower median income than men, leaving them more vulnerable in later life. (Morgan Stanley)
- Women are 80% more likely than men to live in poverty after age 65. (National Institute on Retirement Security)
- Retirement can erode one's sense of purpose but people who maintain a strong sense of meaning live up to seven years longer. (Time)

For many women, retirement is not just about leisure; it's about survival and reinvention. It can also be a powerful season of thriving.

Women who approach retirement with intentionality, planning for financial stability, rediscovering passions, and anchoring themselves in purpose are more likely to experience joy and longevity.

——————— *Pivot Story Spotlight* ———————

Carolyn worked in healthcare for nearly 35 years. When she retired, she was initially thrilled at the thought of rest.

However, within six months, she admitted to feeling rest-less.

"I didn't miss the stress," she said, "but I missed being useful."

So Carolyn began volunteering at a local clinic once a week. She also joined a book club and started gardening. Before long, her days were full again, not with deadlines, but with purpose.

"I realized retirement isn't about stopping," she told me. "It's about shifting. I'm not done making an impact. I'm just doing it differently."

Reflection Prompts

1. What fears do I have about retirement, financial, emotional, or social?

2. What dreams or passions have I set aside that I now have space to explore?

3. How can I stay connected to purpose, meaning, and community in this season?

4. What rhythms (daily, weekly, monthly) will help me thrive after stepping away from full-time work?

Tool: The Purposeful Retirement Plan

This tool helps you design a retirement to help you create a life you love.

Step 1: Financial Check-In
Review savings, income streams, and expenses. Do you need to adjust your lifestyle or explore part-time/free-lance opportunities?

Step 2: Purpose Inventory

List activities that bring you meaning (mentoring, volunteering, creative pursuits, travel, caregiving).

Step 3: Connection Map

Who will you stay connected with? Identify friends, family, or groups to invest in.

Step 4: Health Priorities

Create a wellness rhythm: exercise, preventive care, mindfulness practices.

Step 5: Create Your Ideal Week

Sketch out a balanced weekly rhythm that includes rest, purpose, connection, and fun.

Closing Encouragement

Retirement is about what you're stepping into. Yes, the statistics are sobering. But you have the power to write a different story.

By planning intentionally and anchoring yourself in purpose, this season can be one of joy, freedom, and deep fulfillment.

As you approach or embrace retirement, ask: What am I retiring to?

Thriving isn't about ending a chapter; it's about beginning a new one.

PART II

FOUNDATIONS FOR THRIVING

CHAPTER 6

Thoughts: Reframing the Story You Tell Yourself

When I walked into my first corporate role, I didn't bring my whole self with me. As a young Black woman in predominantly white spaces, I believed success meant code-switching. It meant altering my tone of voice, straightening my hair to appear "professional," smiling when I wanted to frown, and being extra cautious about what I said in meetings. I felt like if I slipped up, it wouldn't just reflect on me but on every other Black woman who might come after me. That's a heavy weight to carry.

I remember one meeting where I had a great idea. I rehearsed it in my head multiple times before speaking. My heart pounded as I finally raised my voice, only to be met with silence and blank stares. A few minutes later, a colleague rephrased the same idea almost exactly, and this time the group praised it. I sat there, shrinking inside, my inner voice whispering, *"See, you don't belong here."*

On the outside, I looked polished. On the inside, I was fighting an invisible battle with my thoughts every single day.

Maybe you've been there, too. Maybe you've just graduated and stepped into your first big girl job. Or maybe you're mid-career, still waiting for someone to validate that you belong. You second-guess yourself, downplay your voice, and wonder if you're enough.

Inevitably, I discovered that **the stories we tell ourselves shape the lives we build.**

Insight

Thoughts are the soil of every pivot. If you plant doubt, you'll grow hesitation. If you plant belief, you'll grow courage. And women are especially vulnerable to what researchers call the *confidence gap*. Studies show:

- **75% of women executives** experience imposter syndrome in their careers (KPMG, *Mind the Gap*).
- Men tend to apply for jobs when they meet only 60% of qualifications, while women often wait until they meet **100%** (Harvard Business Review).
- Women are less likely to speak up in meetings, even when they know the answer, because of fear of judgment (McKinsey, *Women in the Workplace*).

Of course, women don't lack skill or talent. It's just that the *story in our heads* tells us we're not ready, not enough, or don't belong.

The danger is that unchallenged thoughts become self-fulfilling. You believe you're not qualified → you don't apply → you miss the opportunity → which seems to prove the thought was true.

But **stories can be rewritten.**

When I shifted my inner narrative from *"I don't belong here"* to *"I bring value no one else can,"* my confidence began to grow. From *"I'm not ready"* to *"I'm prepared to learn,"* my posture in meetings changed. That shift didn't

just impact me; it also changed the way others respond-
ed to me.

Every pivot you'll ever make, college to career, motherhood, career change, empty nest, retirement, starts in the
mind. And you get to choose the story you'll carry with
you.

 ## Pivot Story Spotlight

"Maya" had just graduated with her master's degree and
landed a job at a major consulting firm. On paper, she was
a star. She had excellent grades, internships, and glowing
recommendations. But every morning she woke up thinking, *I don't deserve this job. They only hired me because
I got lucky.*

In her first client meeting, Maya stayed silent while others brainstormed. Later, a colleague shared an idea nearly identical to what she'd been holding back. The client
loved it. Maya sank into her chair, thinking, *That could
have been me.*

Things changed when Maya began practicing a simple
reframe. Instead of *"I don't deserve to be here,"* she re-
peated, *"I earned this seat. My voice matters."*

The next time she walked into a meeting, she shared
her idea confidently. Not only was it well received, but her
manager later told her, "I'm glad you spoke up. That was
exactly what we needed."

What changed? Not her résumé. Not her skills. Just her
thoughts.

Reflection Prompts

Take a moment to sit with these questions:

1. What's one recurring thought you've been telling yourself in this season?

2. How does this thought shape the way you show up? Does it shrink you, fuel you, or silence you?

3. Who would you be without this thought? What would you do differently?

4. What story would you *choose* to tell yourself instead?

Tool: The Thought Reframe Framework

Here's a step-by-step practice you can use anytime a limiting thought creeps in.

Step 1: Identify the Thought
Write down the exact phrase.

- Example: *"I'm not qualified."*

Step 2: Examine the Evidence
Ask: Is this a fact or a feeling? What evidence disproves this thought?

- Example: *"I've completed the degree, have internship experience, and was chosen for this role."*

Step 3: Reframe the Thought
Turn it into a true statement that is empowering and forward-focused.

- Example: *"I may not know everything yet, but I am qualified and capable of learning what I don't know."*

Step 4: Anchor the Thought
Write your new statement where you'll see it daily, such

as on a sticky note, your phone's wallpaper, or in your planner. Speak it out loud until it feels natural.

Step 5: Practice Across Pivots
Use this exercise in every stage of transition:

- **College to Career:** *"I'm too young to lead."* → *"I bring fresh perspectives and I'm ready to grow."*

- **Motherhood:** *"I'll never balance it all."* → *"I can create rhythms that work for me and my family."*

- **Career Change:** *"It's too late for me."* → *"My experience equips me for this next chapter."*

- **Empty Nest:** *"I'm not needed anymore."* → *"I now have the freedom to rediscover myself."*

- **Retirement:** *"My purpose is over."* → *"This is the beginning of a new legacy."*

Closing Encouragement

When I stopped telling myself I had to be someone else to succeed, everything changed. I stopped shrinking in rooms, started speaking with clarity, and realized that my authentic self was powerful.

You may not be able to control every circumstance but you can control the story you tell yourself about who you are. And when your story changes, your life follows.

As you step into your next transition, ask yourself: *What story am I planting? One of doubt, or one of courage?*

Whatever you plant will grow.

CHAPTER 7

Health & Wellness: Leading with Energy, Not Exhaustion

When my daughters, Kendall and Jalyn, were little, my calendar was chaos. There were work meetings, deadlines, conference calls, school drop-offs, daycare pickups, doctor appointments, dinner to cook, laundry to fold, and a house that always seemed one step away from falling apart. And layered on top of all that was the voice in my head whispering that I had to be everything to everyone. Perfect employee. Perfect mother. Perfect wife. Perfect daughter.

I remember one season when the pressure became unbearable. I was juggling multiple work projects, trying to stay present for my girls, and still saying "yes" to every request. I told myself I could handle it, but the truth was, I was drowning.

One night, after everyone went to bed, I sat down and wrote a letter to my boss. My hands shook as I typed. I didn't sugarcoat it. I admitted I was overwhelmed, that the workload was more than one person could manage, and that I couldn't keep going at this pace. Hitting "send" felt like admitting defeat. I was terrified of being seen as weak, uncommitted, or incapable.

But to my surprise, the response wasn't judgment but compassion. My boss acknowledged my honesty, reassigned part of the workload, and encouraged me to set clearer boundaries.

That experience taught me an invaluable lesson: **speaking up about your limits isn't a weakness, it's wisdom.**

Still, it took me years to truly believe that. Like so many women, I had absorbed the lie that exhaustion was normal, even admirable. That being constantly tired somehow proved I was strong, committed, worthy. However, the truth is that burnout doesn't make us better. It breaks us.

That's why this chapter is all about reclaiming your health and wellness, because your pivot cannot be sustained if you don't have the energy to carry it forward.

Insight

For women, especially mothers, the pressure to do it all is relentless. And it takes a toll.

- **43% of highly qualified women** leave or scale back after having children (Forbes, Harvard Business Review study).

- **1 in 3 mothers** say they've considered downshifting their careers or leaving the workforce entirely during high-stress seasons (McKinsey, *Women in the Workplace*).

- Chronic stress and lack of rest increase the risk of anxiety, depression, and physical illness (American Psychological Association).

We glorify busyness in our culture. How often do we answer "How are you?" with "Busy!" as if that word itself is proof of value? For women, the cultural script is even sharper. We're expected to be the ones who hold everything together. The mental load of remembering school picture days, planning meals, scheduling doctor appointments, and still excelling at work is invisible labor that drains us long before the workday even begins.

Health and wellness are not just about kale smoothies or gym memberships. They are about protecting the energy that fuels your life. They are about rhythms, not just routines. And they are about boundaries, not just busyness.

Every pivot, whether it's motherhood, a career change, or stepping into a leadership role, will test your energy. And if you don't learn to protect it, the pivot will drain you instead of grow you.

I had to learn that my wellness isn't optional, it's foundational. That saying "yes" to my health often meant saying "no" to other things. That rest was not a reward I earned but a rhythm I needed.

And when I learned that, everything shifted.

 *Pivot Story Spotlight*

Danielle was a new mother, six months postpartum, working full-time in a demanding corporate job. She felt like she was failing at everything. Her baby wasn't sleeping through the night. She barely had time to shower. And at work, she was convinced her colleagues saw her as "less committed" now that she was a mom.

Danielle's solution? Push harder. Stay up later. Answer emails at midnight to prove she was still dedicated. Skip meals. Forget exercise. Coffee became her lifeline.

When asked, "What if your energy is your most valuable asset?" she laughed.

But slowly, she began to shift. She started with one boundary: no work emails after 7 p.m. She then asked her partner to handle bedtime two nights a week so she could walk alone, breathe, and reset. She also began meal prepping simple, nourishing food.

Within a month, she said, "I feel like I can breathe again." She was still busy but she wasn't burned out. Her wellness became the anchor that allowed her to show up as both the mother and professional she wanted to be.

Reflection Prompts

Take a few moments with these questions in your journal:

1. How do I currently define wellness in my life? Is it based on how I look or how I feel?
2. Where am I pushing myself to exhaustion in order to prove my worth?
3. What rhythms (rest, movement, nourishment, connection) make me feel most alive?
4. If my energy is my most valuable asset, how would I treat it differently?

Tool: The Energy Audit

Here's a practical exercise to help you lead with energy, not exhaustion:

Step 1: Identify Energy Givers and Drainers

- On one page of your journal, make two columns: Gives Energy and Drains Energy.

- Examples:
  - **Gives:** Walking outside, journaling, meaningful conversations, quality sleep.
  - **Drains:** Scrolling social media, saying yes to things I don't want to do, overcommitting at work.

Step 2: Choose One Small Shift
Pick **ONE** thing you can add to the Gives list and **ONE** thing you can minimize from the Drains list this week.

Step 3: Create a Boundary
Wellness requires boundaries. Decide where you'll draw the line.

- Example: No emails after 7 p.m.
- Example: 20 minutes outside daily, non-negotiable.
- Example: Eight hours of sleep at least three nights per week.

Step 4: Anchor It in Rhythm
Instead of aiming for perfection, think in daily, weekly, and monthly rhythms.

- Daily ➜ Drink more water.
- Weekly ➜ Meal prep Sunday evenings.
- Monthly ➜ Check in with a friend who fills your cup.

Step 5: Revisit and Reset
Review at the end of the month. How's your energy? Where do you feel stronger? Where do you need to reset?

Closing Encouragement

When my girls were little, I thought exhaustion was the price of being a good mom and a good professional. But I've learned that being depleted doesn't serve my children, my work, and especially not me.

Remember this: **Your wellness is not selfish.**

When you protect your health, you protect your dreams. When you honor your rhythms, you sustain your purpose. When you lead with energy, you lead with clarity.

As you step into your next pivot, I want you to ask yourself: *Am I building a life that fuels me, or a life that drains me?*

Thriving isn't about working harder. It's about working smarter from a place of strength.

Resilience: Bouncing Back and Rising Higher

When COVID hit, the world stopped. But my life shifted in a way I didn't expect.

Like millions of women (and men), I was laid off at the beginning of the pandemic. At first, it felt like a rug had been pulled out from under me. I'd built a successful career over 20+ years, and suddenly, I was home, uncertain of what came next.

What surprised me most was not what I lost. It was what I gained.

With no commute and no office deadlines, I started taking daily walks. Nature became my sanctuary. For the first time in years, I noticed the small things: the changing colors of the trees, the rhythm of my own breathing, and the quiet that gave my anxious mind space to settle.

During that season, I also rediscovered something I had once loved, planning. I dusted off my notebooks, grabbed my favorite pens, and found joy in mapping out small, meaningful steps. The best part was that I wasn't doing it alone. My sisters and I created a community of planners. It reminded me of the power of having a village.

Resilience isn't built in isolation. It's built in connection.

As I shared my story on social media, women who had also lost jobs, momentum, or clarity in the middle of uncertainty began reaching out. I then realized resilience isn't just about bouncing back but it's also about rising higher, together.

Insight

Resilience is often described as the ability to bounce back. While that's true, real resilience goes a bit further. It includes finding the strength not only to recover from adversity but also to grow through it.

Transitions such as layoffs, illness, caregiving responsibilities, career changes, empty nests, and retirement will test us. They also carry the seeds of reinvention.

Research backs this up:

- **Resilient people are more likely to experience greater life satisfaction and reduced stress** during transitions (*Everyday Health*).

- Adults who intentionally practiced resilience strategies like optimism, gratitude, and connection reported **higher well-being even after setbacks** (National Institutes of Health).

- Women, who often juggle work, family, and caregiving, report **higher stress** compared to men (American Psychological Association).

Setbacks are inevitable, and we will all face disruptions. But resilience isn't about avoiding hardship (that's impossible to do). It's realizing that the losses allow you to rediscover your strength.

Pivot Story Spotlight

Carla spent 15 years building her career in marketing. When her company went through a merger, she was laid off without warning. For weeks, she spiraled in shame, convinced her career was over. "Who's going to hire me at this age?" she asked.

Instead of staying stuck, Carla began journaling every morning. At first, it was just venting. But slowly, her writing turned into more of a reflection. She wrote about what she actually loved about her past work and what she didn't. She made lists of ideas for the future.

Within a few months, she launched her own consulting business, working with small businesses in her community. "Losing that job," she said, "was the best thing that could have happened. It pushed me to build a life I actually love."

Carla's story is proof that resilience isn't about avoiding the fall. It's about how you rise after it.

Reflection Prompt

Take a moment to journal your answers:

1. Think about a setback you've experienced in the past year. How did you respond?
2. What lessons or new strengths did you gain from that experience?
3. Who makes up your village (the people who help you stay grounded in hard times)?
4. What would resilience look like for you in this current season (not just bouncing back, but rising higher)?

Tool: The Four Anchors of Resilience

During my COVID layoff, I discovered four anchors that carried me forward. These can carry you, too.

1. **Beauty**
   Pause to notice what grounds and calms you. For me, it was daily walks in nature. For you, it might be art, music, or quiet mornings.

2. **Purpose**
   Rediscover something that lights you up. I fell back in love with planning and mapping out my days. Purpose doesn't have to be grand. It can be a small spark that keeps you moving.

3. **Community**
   Lean on your village. My village became my lifeline during the COVID-19 pandemic. Who are the people who laugh, cry, and encourage you when life feels heavy?

4. **Service**
   Help others who are navigating the same storm. As I shared my story, other women found hope in it. Sometimes, the best way to heal yourself is to walk alongside someone else who is going through the same thing.

Exercise: Build Your Resilience Rituals

1. **Choose Your Anchor:** Which of the four (Beauty, Purpose, Community, Service) do you most need right now?

2. **Create a Small Ritual:** Decide one way you'll practice it this week.

   - Beauty → 10-minute walk daily.

   - Purpose → Journal one page each morning.

- Community → Call a friend once a week.

- Service → Share a resource or word of encouragement with another woman.

3. **Reflect on the Impact:** After two weeks, ask: How do I feel different? Where do I feel stronger?

Closing Encouragement

When I was laid off during the COVID-19 pandemic, I gained something I didn't expect: resilience. I gained the ability to find beauty in simple walks, the joy of rediscovering old passions, the comfort of leaning on my village, and the purpose of helping other women rise.

Resilience isn't about going back to who you were before. It's about becoming who you're meant to be next.

When life knocks you down, ask yourself: *What anchors can I lean on? How can I rise higher because of this?*

Thriving through transitions isn't about never falling. It's about always rising.

CHAPTER 9

Identity: Rediscovering Who You Are Beyond the Roles

For years in my corporate career, I wore a mask. Not a physical one. The kind you can't see.

Every morning, before walking into the office, I practiced my smile, changed my tone of voice, and carefully chose an outfit that looked "professional." I code-switched, softened my opinions, and made sure not to take up too much space. Underneath that mask, my thoughts whispered, "Don't mess up. Don't be too loud. Don't give them a reason to say you don't belong."

I was good at the role I played. From the outside, I looked confident, successful, and put together. But on the inside, I felt invisible. My true self (my humor, my creativity, my unique perspective) wasn't showing up. And the more I hid behind that mask, the more I lost sight of who I was.

Maybe you've felt this too. As women, we take on so many roles: mother, daughter, leader, wife, caregiver, and professional. Somewhere along the way, our identity gets tangled up in them. We forget who we are outside of what we *do* for everyone else.

For me, the turning point came when I realized that hiding my identity didn't make me safer; it made me smaller.

And smaller wasn't serving me, or the people I was called to impact.

The day I started showing up as my authentic, unapologetic, and unmasked self was the day everything began to change.

Insight

Identity is one of the most powerful forces shaping our choices and our pivots. When we don't know who we are, we cling to roles, titles, or expectations to define us. But roles change. Careers end. Children grow up. Relationships shift. And when they do, women often ask: *Who am I now?*

Research shows:

- During major transitions, such as motherhood, career change, or empty nesting, women negotiate between their past selves and emerging selves. (**Gender, Work, & Organization**)

- Women's sense of self often shifts dramatically during motherhood, as they renegotiate professional, personal, and domestic identities. (**Journal of Reproductive and Infant Psychology**)

Identity evolves over time. Every transition is an invitation to peel back the layers of roles and rediscover who you are at the core.

For me, that meant realizing I was more than a job title. More than Jalyn and Kendall's mom. I am a woman called to thrive authentically, and to help other women do the same.

 *Pivot Story Spotlight*

Angela spent 25 years of her life as a devoted mother. When her youngest left for college, she felt proud, but also lost. "For years," she said, "my identity was wrapped up in being needed. Now, I walk into a quiet house and wonder: Who am I if I'm not somebody's mom every day?"

Angela began working through an identity rediscovery exercise. She listed qualities that had nothing to do with her roles: creative, compassionate, adventurous, resourceful. She started painting again, something she hadn't done in decades.

Within a year, Angela launched a small online art business, selling pieces that celebrated women in transition. "I thought I was losing myself," she said, "but really, I was finding her again."

Angela's story is a reminder that pivots can strip away old roles but they also reveal hidden parts of ourselves waiting to shine.

Reflection Prompts

Grab your journal and reflect:

1. What roles do I currently hold (mother, leader, partner, caregiver, etc.)?
2. Who am I outside of those roles? What qualities, strengths, or passions define me?
3. When was the last time I felt most like myself? What was I doing? Who was I with?
4. What parts of me have I been hiding or minimizing?

Tool: Identity Reclamation Map

Use this exercise to begin rediscovering your authentic self.

Step 1: List Your Roles
Write down every role you currently hold (e.g., mom, leader, sister, volunteer).

Step 2: Separate "Role" from "Self"
For each role, ask: Which of my qualities show up in this role? Example: As a mother, I am nurturing and creative.

Step 3: Identify Core Qualities
Circle the qualities that show up across multiple roles. These are likely part of your core identity.

Step 4: Reclaim Hidden Parts
Think of something you've stopped doing because of life's demands. Write one way to reintroduce it into your life.

Step 5: Write Your "I Am" Statement
Craft a statement that reflects your authentic self, beyond roles.

- Example: *I am a woman of resilience, creativity, and faith. I bring joy and clarity wherever I go.*

Closing Encouragement

Your identity isn't limited to the roles you hold or the expectations others place on you. You are more than that. Every transition, whether it's motherhood, empty nest, or retirement, is an invitation to rediscover who you've always been.

You don't have to wait for someone else to define you. You get to define yourself.

Take off the mask, reclaim your voice, and step into your next chapter as your authentic self.

CHAPTER 10

Vision: Designing the Next Chapter with Intention

For as long as I can remember, I've been a dreamer. Even in the busiest seasons of life, I've carried a vision of what I want my future to look like. Here's what I see:

My husband, Lavell, and I are living in a luxury high-rise condo in a major city. We're in a walkable neighborhood with easy access to public transportation. We travel the world together, exploring new cultures, food, and history. I'm speaking on stages across the globe, empowering women, consulting with organizations, and leading workshops that help people reset and realign with their purpose. Financially, we're comfortable; our needs are met, our future is secure, and we're able to give generously to causes we believe in.

This is not just a dream. It's a picture of intention because vision doesn't just happen. It's created. If we don't design our lives with intention, we end up living by default instead of by design.

Every pivot, whether it's starting a new career, becoming an empty nester, or stepping into retirement, is a chance to pause, dream again, and ask: *Where am I going, and who am I becoming?*

Insight

Vision is the compass that guides your pivots. Without it, transitions feel disorienting. With it, even challenges can feel purposeful.

Research underscores the importance of vision:

- People who think about their future make better choices today. (Psychology Today)
- Life-crafting (writing out your goals, commitments, and future plans) leads to significant increases in meaning, purpose, and goal attainment over time. (Frontiers in Psychology)

These findings confirm what many women feel: without vision, transitions can leave us feeling adrift, financially insecure, emotionally disconnected, or struggling to re-discover purpose.

But when you approach transitions with intentionality, you reclaim agency. Vision empowers you to design a future aligned with your values, passions, and priorities.

—————————  *Pivot Story Spotlight* —————————

Sandra spent 30 years working in education. When she retired at 62, she thought she'd finally rest. However, within months, she began to feel restless. "I miss having a reason to get up every morning," she admitted.

Through coaching, Sandra began envisioning her next chapter. She realized she loved mentoring younger women and had a lifelong passion for travel. With intentional planning, she started a small consultancy for new teachers and joined a volunteer program that allowed her to teach abroad for part of the year.

Sandra's retirement no longer felt like an ending. It became a new chapter of purpose.

"I may not have a regular job anymore," she said, "but I'm still building a legacy."

Her story is proof that vision isn't just about money or status. It's about meaning.

Reflection Prompts

Pause and reflect on these questions:

1. When I picture my ideal next chapter, what do I see? Who's there with me?
2. What values do I want to guide this season of my life?
3. What fears are holding me back from envisioning boldly?
4. If I designed my future with intention, what would change about how I live today?

Tool: The Vision Casting Framework

Use this framework to design your future with clarity.

Step 1: Dream It
Close your eyes and imagine your ideal future. Where are you living? What does your day look like? Who's around you?

Step 2: Plan It
Put your vision in words. Be specific. Instead of "I want to travel," write "I want to spend two weeks a year exploring new countries."

Step 3: Align with Your Values
Ask: Does this vision reflect what matters most to me? Identify 3–5 values (e.g., family, faith, health, freedom, impact).

Step 4: Identify Gaps
Where are you now vs. where you want to be? What financial, personal, or professional gaps need to be addressed?

Step 5: Do It
Break your vision into small, doable steps.

- Example: Open a travel savings account.

- Example: Join a speaker's bureau to increase visibility.

- Example: Block one evening a week for date nights with your spouse.

Step 6: Share It
Tell someone you trust about your vision. Accountability strengthens follow-through.

Closing Encouragement

A vision is more than a dream. It's a roadmap. Whether you're entering a new job, transitioning to an empty nest, or stepping into retirement, your vision will determine whether you drift or thrive.

Don't wait for life to hand you purpose. Create it.

As you design your next chapter, remember that **you are never too old, too late, or too stuck to dream again.**

Look ahead with intention. Write the story only you can live.

CHAPTER 11

Execution: Turning Vision into Courageous Action

When I first started envisioning life beyond my 9–5, I had a clear picture that included traveling the world as a keynote speaker, building THRIVE Consulting into a thriving business, and coaching women to live life on purpose with purpose.

I had journals full of ideas, sticky notes plastered with goals, and late-night planning sessions. Yet nothing changed until I started taking action.

The first steps weren't (and still aren't) glamorous. The steps looked like working later to write after work and saying no to opportunities that weren't aligned with my vision. It also meant booking small speaking engagements, even though my dream was to keynote at conferences.

I learned that **execution isn't about giant leaps. It's about consistent, courageous steps.**

Here's the part most people miss: action doesn't eliminate fear. When I sent my first pitch to an organization, I was terrified. When I launched She Thrives Collective, I wondered, "What if no one joins?" But every small step built momentum.

Execution is where faith meets discipline. It's the bridge between the life you imagine and the one you actually live.

Insight

We often believe success comes from inspiration or motivation. But research shows it's daily habits and small actions that create lasting change.

> "Habits, not motivation, are the strongest predictors of long-term success, because willpower is limited, but systems sustain momentum." (Atomic Habits by James Clear)

Execution isn't about being perfect or fearless; it's about creating systems that make courage easier and action automatic.

When women embrace execution, they move from dreaming to building. From wishing to walking. From hoping to thriving.

 ——————— *Pivot Story Spotlight* ———————

Marissa dreamed of starting a nonprofit to mentor teenage girls. For years, she journaled about it, talked about it, and prayed about it. But fear of failure kept her stuck.

One day, she decided to execute one small step: host a free Saturday workshop at her church for 10 girls. She borrowed space, printed flyers at home, and used her own story as the teaching material.

That workshop changed everything. Parents asked when the next session would be. Volunteers offered to help. Within a year, she had a nonprofit, a board of directors, and a regular mentoring program.

Marissa didn't start with a full business plan or a big budget. She started with action.

Reflection Prompts

1. What vision am I holding onto that I haven't acted on yet?
2. What's one small step I can take this week toward that vision?
3. What fears have been keeping me from execution? How can I reframe them?
4. Who can I share my goals with for accountability?

Tool: The Execution Ladder

Use this ladder to move from vision to reality.

Step 1: Define Your Goal
Write down a clear, specific outcome.

- Example: *I want to feel healthier and more energized by building a consistent wellness routine.*

Step 2: Break It Down
List the milestones that lead to your goal.

- Example: *Drink more water, move my body 3x per week, meal prep simple lunches, and set a regular bedtime.*

Step 3: Schedule the Steps
Block time in your calendar for each action.

- Example: *Put workouts on your calendar like meetings. Set a daily phone reminder for 10 p.m. bedtime.*

Step 4: Build Accountability
Share your steps with someone you trust.

- Example: *Ask a friend to text you after their workout, so you can check in with yours. Or join a walking group.*

Step 5: Celebrate Progress
Mark small wins along the way.

- Example: *After 2 weeks of consistent sleep, treat yourself to fresh flowers or a new journal.*

Step 6: Repeat and Refine
Review what worked, adjust what didn't, and keep moving forward.

- Example: *Maybe morning workouts aren't realistic, so shift to evenings. The key is progress, not perfection.*

Closing Encouragement

Execution isn't glamorous. Early mornings, late nights, small risks, and steady steps are where transformation happens.

The life you envision is waiting for you but it won't just arrive. You build it. Step by step. Decision by decision. Action by action.

So take the leap. Write the email. Pitch the idea. Book the ticket. Launch the program.

Thriving doesn't happen in the dreaming. It happens in the doing.

PART III

THRIVING IN COMMUNITY & LEADERSHIP

CHAPTER 12

Faith, Purpose, and Calling: Anchoring in Something Bigger

The story of Mary and Martha in Luke 10:38–42 has always resonated with me. In the passage, Jesus visits their home. Martha is busy preparing, serving, and trying to make sure everything is perfect. Mary, on the other hand, sits at Jesus' feet, listening.

Frustrated, Martha complains that she's doing all the work while Mary just sits. But Jesus gently tells her, *"Martha, you are worried and upset about many things, but few things are needed, or indeed only one. Mary has chosen what is better, and it will not be taken away from her."*

I think about this story often, because I've lived it.

There have been seasons when I've been Martha, busy, overwhelmed, trying to keep everything together, making sure everyone else is cared for while I run on empty. And there have been seasons when I've been Mary, choosing presence over performance, purpose over pressure, peace over perfection.

The Mary & Martha story is about faith and focus. It's about anchoring your life in something bigger than the endless to-do lists and shifting transitions. When you root yourself in purpose and calling, you find clarity even in the middle of chaos.

Insight

Faith, purpose, and calling are practical anchors for thriving in transitions. When women anchor themselves in something bigger than their circumstances, they build resilience, clarity, and hope. This is a biblical truth.

- Faith provides direction when life feels uncertain. *"Trust in the Lord with all your heart and lean not on your own understanding; in all your ways submit to him, and he will make your paths straight."* Proverbs 3:5–6 (NIV)

- Purpose reminds us that our lives are designed with intention.*"For we are God's handiwork, created in Christ Jesus to do good works, which God prepared in advance for us to do."* Ephesians 2:10 (NIV)

Calling affirms that our pivots are part of God's plan. *"And we know that in all things God works for the good of those who love him, who have been called according to his purpose."* Romans 8:28 (NIV)

Together, these truths remind us that **faith steadies us, purpose directs us, and calling moves us forward.** Anchoring in these three pillars provides the clarity, courage, and peace to thrive.

 *Pivot Story Spotlight*

Sharon had just gone through a major career transition. She was uncertain about her future and worried she had missed her chance to make an impact. However, during a coaching session, she shared how volunteering at her church had given her a sense of joy she hadn't felt in years.

"That's my calling," she realized. "Helping women through prayer and encouragement."

Sharon didn't launch a new business or return to corporate life. Instead, she built a ministry of presence, mentoring younger women, creating a prayer group, and supporting families in need.

Her story reminds us that purpose doesn't always show up as a paycheck. Sometimes it shows up as a life poured out in service.

Reflection Prompts

1. When do I feel most connected to something bigger than myself?
2. What activities or moments give me a deep sense of meaning and fulfillment?
3. How does my faith (or personal belief system) influence the way I navigate transitions?
4. What do I sense I'm being called to in this current season?

Tool: Purpose Inventory & Alignment Checklist

Step 1: Purpose Inventory
Write down 5 moments in your life when you felt most alive, fulfilled, or connected. What themes show up?

Step 2: Calling Statement
Craft a simple statement that captures your sense of calling.

- Example: *"I am called to encourage and equip women to thrive in every season."*

Step 3: Alignment Check
Review your current commitments. Are they aligned with your calling? Where are you spending time out of obligation vs. purpose?

Step 4: Reset Your Focus
Decide on one way to realign your week with your sense of calling.

- Example: Block 30 minutes for prayer or reflection each morning.

- Example: Volunteer in an area that connects to your passion.

Step 5: Anchor It in Faith
Choose a grounding practice, prayer, meditation, journaling, or service that keeps you connected to your purpose.

Closing Encouragement

Transitions will always bring uncertainty. But when your life is anchored in faith, purpose, and calling, you're never adrift.

Like Mary, you can choose presence over pressure. Like Martha, you can still get things done without losing sight of what matters most.

Your calling is not limited to a role, a job, or a season. It's the thread that runs through your entire life.

When you feel overwhelmed by the pivot you're facing, ask yourself: *What is my "better part"? What is the one thing I'm being called to choose today?*

Anchoring in something bigger gives you the clarity, courage, and peace to thrive through them.

CHAPTER 13

The Power of Community and Sisterhood

When the world shut down at the beginning of COVID, I felt like the rug had been pulled out from under me. I didn't have a job, and like many people, I was trying to figure out a new normal.

In the midst of that uncertainty, something beautiful and unexpected happened. Every day, I went for walks outside. Nature became my therapy, my prayer room, and my reset button. And along the way, I started sharing more of my story about being laid off, rediscovering what mattered, and creating space for joy. So many women leaned in, and together we built a rhythm of connection.

We reminded one another that we weren't alone.

Thriving isn't something we do in isolation. It's something we do in community.

Those encounters planted the seeds for what would become *She Thrives Collective*, a space where women could come together across generations and life stages to lift each other up.

Insight

Community and sisterhood are lifelines. Research and scripture show that women thrive when they are connected:

- Loneliness increases the risk of premature death by 26%. (*Department of Health & Human Services*)
- Women with strong social ties tend to have better mental health, lower stress levels, and higher resilience. (World Psychiatry)
- Ecclesiastes 4:9–10 puts it simply: "Two are better than one, because they have a good return for their labor: If either of them falls down, one can help the other up."

Thriving in sisterhood means having women who see you, hear you, and walk with you.

 ——— *Pivot Story Spotlight* ———

Angela was a high-achieving executive who, on paper, had everything together. But inside, she felt isolated. She didn't think she could be vulnerable with her colleagues, and she didn't want to burden her family.

It wasn't until she joined a women's mastermind group that she realized how much she needed community. For the first time, she felt safe admitting her fears. She found encouragement, wisdom, and accountability.

"That group saved me," Angela confessed. "I didn't just find friends; I found sisters."

Her story reminds us: sisterhood is more than social. It's transformational.

Reflection Prompts

1. Who are the women I can call when life feels heavy?
2. What fears hold me back from leaning on others for support?
3. How have I experienced the power of community in the past?
4. What kind of sisterhood do I want to create or be part of in this season?

Tool: The Community Map

This tool will help you identify and strengthen the circles of community that sustain you.

Step 1: List Your Circles
Identify your current communities (family, friends, co-workers, church, groups).

Step 2: Evaluate the Health
Next to each, write: Does this circle energize me, drain me, or support me?

Step 3: Spot the Gaps
What's missing? Do you need more encouragement, accountability, or shared purpose?

Step 4: Build Intentional Connections
Decide on one step to strengthen your sisterhood this month.

- Example: Start a monthly brunch with friends.

- Example: Join a local or online women's group.

Step 5: Be the Sister You Need
Commit to checking in on one woman in your circle this week. Sometimes the best way to build community is to model it.

Closing Encouragement

You were never meant to thrive alone. Sisterhood makes the challenges of life lighter. While community doesn't solve every problem, it reminds you that you don't have to face them by yourself.

So, lean into your sisters. Build your circles. Be intentional about creating spaces where women can show up fully and unapologetically.

Thriving is a collective journey. And together, we can go further.

PART IV

MASTERING THE PIVOT WITH THRIVE

CHAPTER 14

The Pivot Playbook: Applying THRIVE to Any Transition

When I first developed the THRIVE framework, it wasn't a business idea; it was survival.

I had gone through seasons of overwhelm, toxic workplaces, motherhood transitions, and even being laid off. Every time, I kept asking myself, '*How do I keep going? How do I move forward when life feels uncertain?*'

As I reflected on what helped me grow stronger, I realized it always came back to six anchors: my thoughts, my health, my resilience, my identity, my vision, and my execution. That became the THRIVE framework.

Since then, I've coached women, spoken to leaders, and built communities around these six pillars. And I've seen it over and over again: when women apply THRIVE, they don't just survive transitions, they transform through them.

This chapter is about giving you the playbook, your step-by-step guide for applying THRIVE to any pivot, big or small.

Insight

Transitions come in all shapes and sizes: a new job, a new city, motherhood, divorce, retirement, even rediscovering yourself after burnout. The circumstances differ, but the principles of thriving remain the same.

That's where THRIVE comes in.

- **Thoughts:** Your mindset determines your ability to see possibilities instead of roadblocks.

- **Health & Wellness:** Protecting and replenishing your energy sustains you in the long run.

- **Resilience:** Learning to bounce back from setbacks builds strength for the next chapter.

- **Identity:** Knowing who you are beyond roles or titles helps you stay grounded.

- **Vision:** Designing a future you want gives you direction when life feels uncertain.

- **Execution:** Turning ideas into small, consistent actions makes transformation possible.

People who have frameworks or strategies for transitions are more likely to succeed. For example, goal-setting theory demonstrates that individuals with clear, specific goals achieve significantly more than those with vague intentions (Positive Psychology).

The THRIVE framework works the same way; it gives structure and clarity when everything else feels in flux.

Case Studies

Case Study 1: The Career Change

- *Before:* Jessica was stuck in a corporate job that paid well but left her drained.

- *THRIVE Applied:* She reframed her thoughts around fear, improved her wellness by setting boundaries, built resilience by learning new skills, redefined her identity beyond her title, cast a vision for nonprofit leadership, and executed by networking and applying.

- *After:* Within a year, she pivoted into a purpose-driven role.

Case Study 2: The New Mother

- *Before:* Priya felt guilty all the time, both at work and at home.

- *THRIVE Applied:* She reframed her thoughts around "perfect mother" expectations, created a health rhythm with rest breaks, built resilience through support groups, reclaimed her identity as both professional and mom, envisioned balance, and executed with boundary-setting conversations.

- *After:* She found a rhythm that worked for her family and career.

Case Study 3: The Retiree

- *Before:* Maria retired after 40 years in education and suddenly felt lost without a classroom.

- *THRIVE Applied:* She reframed her thoughts around irrelevance, focusing on wellness through walking and gardening, leaned on resilience from past challenges, redefined her identity as a mentor instead of a teacher, cast a vision of volunteering, and executed it by joining a literacy nonprofit.

- *After:* She found renewed purpose and joy in giving back.

Reflection Prompts

1. Which of the THRIVE pillars feels strongest for me right now? Which feels weakest?
2. How have I already used parts of THRIVE in past transitions without realizing it?
3. What transition am I currently navigating, and how could THRIVE guide me through it?
4. Who could I invite into my journey for accountability and encouragement?

Tool: The THRIVE Self-Assessment & Coaching Toolkit

Step 1: Rate Yourself
Score yourself 1–10 in each THRIVE pillar (Thoughts, Health, Resilience, Identity, Vision, Execution).

Step 2: Identify Your Focus
Which two areas are lowest? These become your priority growth areas.

Step 3: Pick One Action
For each weak area, choose one practical action.

- Example: If Health is low → add a daily 20-minute walk.

- Example: If Vision is low → write a 1-page description of your ideal next chapter.

Step 4: Build Accountability
Share your THRIVE focus with a friend, coach, or group.

Step 5: Reassess Regularly
Repeat the assessment every 90 days to track growth and stay aligned.

Closing Encouragement

The pivots in your life will keep coming. You may not control when or how they show up but you *can* control how you respond.

The THRIVE framework is a compass. It gives you a way to move through transitions with clarity, courage, and confidence.

The next time life throws a pivot your way, don't panic. Pick up this playbook. Walk through the six pillars. And remind yourself that you have everything you need to thrive.

CHAPTER 15

Common Detours and How to Get Back on Track

'll never forget the time I thought I had everything lined up perfectly. I had the plan, the calendar, the deadlines, the energy; I was clicking on all cylinders. But within weeks, everything unraveled.

A project at work went sideways, one of my girls had an accident that required surgery and physical therapy, and suddenly, the hours I thought I had available disappeared. I felt like I was failing before I had even really started.

What I realized in that season was that the problem wasn't the detour. The problem was that I didn't have a way to reset. Once I learned to pause, reframe, and start again, the detours no longer felt like part of the journey.

Pivots rarely happen in a straight line. There are always detours, fear, fatigue, financial strain, expectations from others, and even our own inner critic. The key is learning how to get back on track.

Insight

Here are some of the most common detours women face during transitions:

- **Fear of the Unknown**
  Fear can paralyze progress. Studies show that fear of failure can stunt career growth (Forbes).

- **Overcommitment**
  Women are more likely to struggle with balancing work and family, making it harder for them to advance in their careers. (Pew Research Center).

- **Financial Pressure**
  Money is one of the biggest barriers to making transitions. 90% of Americans report financial concerns as their top source of stress (CNBC).

- **Cultural or Family Expectations**
  From being the perfect mother to staying in secure jobs, societal and family norms often pressure women to stay in roles that no longer serve them.

Detours don't mean dead ends. With the right practices, you can reset, regain clarity, and continue forward.

 *Pivot Story Spotlight*

Renee wanted to start a business after years in corporate, but every time she took a step forward, fear held her back. "What if I fail? What if people laugh at me? What if I lose everything?"

Through coaching, Renee learned to identify her fear triggers and replace them with resilience practices. She created a financial plan, leaned on her support system, and reminded herself of her "why."

Today, Renee runs a thriving consulting practice. She admits the detours are still there but she now has the tools to get back on track.

Reflection Prompts

1. Which detour shows up most often in my life (fear, overcommitment, finances)?
2. How do I usually respond when I feel off track?
3. What practices help me reset and regain clarity?
4. Who can I lean on for support when I'm stuck?

Tool: Reset Practices & Pivot-Pause Worksheet

The Pivot Pause

When you feel stuck, use this 5-step reset:

1. **Pause** – Take a breath. Step back before reacting.
2. **Name It** – Identify the detour (fear, overcommitment, finances).
3. **Reframe It** – Ask: What's the opportunity here? What can this teach me?
4. **Plan It** – Choose one small next step.
5. **Move Forward** – Take action, no matter how small.

Resilience Mantras

Write down affirmations to keep you grounded during detours:

- *"A detour is not a dead end."*
- *"I am equipped for this pivot."*
- *"Progress, not perfection, moves me forward."*
- *"My pace is still progress."*

Worksheet

- Current Detour: _____

- How It Shows Up: _____

- What It's Teaching Me: _____

- My Next Step: _____

Closing Encouragement

Every pivot comes with detours. But the detour doesn't define your destination.

Fear will whisper. Finances will weigh heavy. Expectations will press in. None of those is stronger than your resilience, your vision, and your calling.

When you find yourself off track, remember that you don't need to start over. You just need to pause, reset, and take the next step forward.

Thriving is about learning how to rise, again and again.

CHAPTER 16

Thriving Beyond the Pivot: Creating a Life You Love

I often imagine my future life with Lavell. We're living in a high-rise condo with a view of the city. Public transportation is just a short walk away, and our days are filled with peace, joy, and purpose. I travel the world speaking and consulting, helping women and organizations thrive. And when I come home, I'm grounded in a life of love, comfort, and financial freedom.

That's my vision. It's what keeps me moving forward when the pivots get hard.

Your pivots are about creating the life you want to live. Every step, every transition, every reset adds up to the story of your becoming.

Thriving beyond the pivot doesn't mean life is perfect. It means life is intentional. It means you've learned to embrace change not as a threat but as an opportunity to grow into the next version of yourself.

Insight

The pivots you face are stepping stones.

Research shows that people who reflect on their growth and intentionally set goals for their future are more likely to experience long-term well-being:

- **Self-reflection and intentional goal-setting are linked to higher resilience and life satisfaction.**
  — Lyubomirsky, S., Sheldon, K. M., & Schkade, D. (2005). *Pursuing Happiness: The Architecture of Sustainable Change.* Review of General Psychology.
  Read here

- **People with a strong sense of purpose report better mental and physical health and even live longer.**
  — Yale School of Public Health.
  Read here

- **Regular reflection rituals, like journaling or annual reviews, improve clarity, reduce stress, and strengthen decision-making.**
  — University of Texas at Austin, *Writing About Emotional Experiences as a Therapeutic Process.*
  Read here

Thriving beyond the pivot means taking what you've learned and building rhythms that keep you aligned with your purpose, no matter what life brings.

———————  *Pivot Story Spotlight* ———————

Elena underwent multiple pivots in a short period, including sending her kids to college, caring for her aging parents, and stepping back from a demanding job. At first, she felt disoriented.

"I kept asking, 'Who am I now?'" she shared.

Instead of staying stuck, Elena began creating new rituals. She journaled weekly, joined a women's community, and started volunteering at an organization that aligned with her passions. Within a year, she felt more grounded than ever because she was living with intention.

Her story reminds us that thriving is about using pivots to become who you were always meant to be.

Reflection Prompts

1. What does my ideal thriving life look like?
2. How have the pivots in my past prepared me for the future I want to create?
3. What rhythms or rituals can I commit to that will keep me aligned with my purpose?
4. Who do I want alongside me in the next chapter of my journey?

Tool: The Annual Pivot Review

A practical rhythm to keep you aligned year after year.

Step 1: Look Back

- What were my biggest pivots this year?

- What did I learn from them?

Step 2: Celebrate Growth

- List 3 ways I grew stronger, wiser, or more resilient this year.

Step 3: Reset Alignment

- Using the THRIVE pillars, where am I strongest? Where do I need more focus?

Step 4: Cast Vision

- Write a one-page vision for the next year. What do I want to step into?

Step 5: Create Action Steps

- Choose 3 concrete goals that align with my vision.

Step 6: Commit and Share

- Share my goals with a trusted friend, mentor, or community for accountability.

Closing Encouragement

As you close this book, I want you to remember that you were not made to just survive transitions. You were made to thrive through them.

Every pivot, whether it's college to career, motherhood, career change, empty nest, retirement, or rediscovering your calling, has shaped you into the woman you are today. And it's another opportunity to grow, realign, and step into the life you were created to live.

So don't fear the pivots. Embrace them. They are the very path to your destiny.

As you walk forward, may you do so with clarity, courage, and a sense of community, building a life you truly love.

ACKNOWLEDGEMENTS

Writing this book reflects not just my own pivots, but the collective wisdom, support, and encouragement of so many people who have walked with me.

First, giving honor, thanks, and praise to God, who has been faithful through every pivot in my life. Every closed door, every new beginning, every lesson learned all point back to Him and His grace.

To my husband, Lavell, thank you for believing in me and for cheering me on in every season. Your steady encouragement reminds me daily that I don't have to do this alone.

To my daughters, Jalyn and Kendall, watching you grow into strong, beautiful, and resilient young women has been one of my greatest joys. You remind me of why I do this work. I want every woman to know that she can thrive in every stage of her journey.

To my Sisters (you all know who you are), thank you for being my village. From walking together during the hardest seasons to laughter that carried me through uncertainty, you showed me the power of community and sisterhood.

And finally, to every woman who has ever felt overwhelmed, unseen, or uncertain about her next step, this book is for you. May you find yourself in these pages. May you hear the whisper of your own strength, your own clarity, and your own calling. And may you know that you were never meant to just survive transitions, you were always meant to thrive through them.